Under Brushstrokes

UNDER BRUSH STROKES

Poems

HEDY HABRA

Press 53
Winston-Salem

Press 53, LLC
PO Box 30314
Winston-Salem, NC 27130

First Edition

SILVER CONCHO POETRY SERIES

Cover design by Paul Sizer

Cover art, "Woman & Lotus," Copyright © 2015 by Hedy Habra

Author photo by Michael T. Lanka

Printed on acid-free paper
ISBN 978-1-941209-23-3

Acknowledgments

Some of these poems have appeared, sometimes in a slightly different version in the following publications:

The Bitter Oleander, "Drop by Drop," "*Face à face*"
Black Tongue Review, "After the Tsunami: The Cherry Tree Laments"
Blue Fifth Review, "Nocturne," "Skin Flashing Where the Garment Gapes"
Change Seven, "The Ages of Woman," "Shipwrecked"
Cider Press Review, "Sounds in the Attic"
Connotation Press, "The Ages of Man," "Initiation," "Musical Score in Pearly Layers"
Cumberland River Review, "The Apple of Granada"
Danse Macabre, "After the Storm," "Afterthought," "Awakening," "Brushstrokes," "Desert Song,"
Diode, "Under the Waterfall"
Duende, "It Takes Two to Tango" (as "Europa's Song")
Drunken Boat, "Obsessive Compulsion"
Grafemas, "Unborn"
The Innisfree Poetry Journal, "The Camisole"
Knot Magazine, "Boreas' Anger," "Expectations," "The Upright Piano"
Museum Views: Art Info, "Goya Dining at *La Quinta del Sordo*," "Mona Lisa," "A Triptych: *Visibile parlare in sotto voce*: I. What the Painter Hears, II. The Artist as Voyeur, III. Before the Storm"
Parting Gifts, "At the Violet Hour," "Flora & the End of the Bird's Song," "Lovers," "Phoenician Twilight," "*Trompe-l'œil*"
Pirene's Fountain, "Behind the Scenes," "Broken Ladder," "The Canary & the Feathered Mask," "The Captive," ' Hiding Under Brushstrokes," "Inside Your Palm," "Insomnia in Sorrento," "Lidless Eyes," "The Memory of Unspoken Words," "Reading at a Table," "Walking Around in Cambodia"
Poet Lore, "On the Sargasso Sea"
Poetic Diversity: The Litzine of Los Angeles, "Encounter in the Yellow Hour"
Prairie Wolf Press, "Inner Voice"
The Smoking Poet, "The Dance," "Origin," "Time Off," "Timing"
Solstice Literary Magazine, "Gezi Park, 2013"
Sulphur River Literary Review, "Under the Crescent Moon," "Walking Around Bernini's *Apollo & Daphne*"

Anthologies

First Water, The Best of Pirene's Fountain, "Broken Ladder"
The Original Van Gogh's Ear, "A Triptych: *Visibile parlare in sotto voce*: I. What the Painter Hears, II. The Artist as Voyeur, III. Before the Storm"
Sunrise from Blue Thunder Japan, "Aftershocks in Fukushima," "Hokusai's *The Great Wave*"

Under Brushstrokes

I.

II.

III.

IV.

V.

VI.

I.

Obsessive Compulsion

I knew a woman who spent hours in front
of her magnifying mirror, chasing split hairs
like a huntress. She'd enter the intricacy of
parallel lines, watch forking tips grow into
reeds, swelling into bamboo shoots painted in
Chinese ink over transparent rice paper through
which she saw her son falling from a cliff, light
as a clipping, he lies at the bottom of the dark
ravine, his foot severed, tshuk tshuk tshuk
crisscross, cuts the slightest twist, he's being
raised with pulleys, in a fog she wanders in
deserted streets unable to find her way back,
she'd forgotten her own name, thinking of her
son's severed foot bleeding, his thick fragrant
blood an oddity in the night scented with
rosemary and lavender, she thinks of mountain
lions, coyotes, a jugular vein prey to canines
sharper than shears, hears feline raspy tongues
licking the wound, refuses to see the man's body
tremble, the tense hardening of muscles prior
to rigor mortis that would come so fast, yes,
he shouldn't suffer she prays, eyes closed, finds
herself back in front of her bathroom mirror
holding the scissors, holding her breath, yes,
it was only an illusion and her son was recovering
now with nails stuck into his leg, surgeons cleaned
the wound nine hours long, gloved hands cut
tshuk tshuk sawed scraps, sewed back tissues
and bones, the rest of him whole, tshuk tshuk tshuk
the crisscrossing cuts the slightest deviance, none
will escape, crisscross she aims, tinkers with precision.

The Apple of Granada

Some say Eve handed a pomegranate to Adam, and it makes sense to me. How can the flesh of an apple compare to the bejeweled juicy garnets, the color of passion, hidden under its elastic pink skin tight as an undersized glove, a fruit withholding the power to doom and exile since the dawn of time. For a few irresistible seeds, didn't Persephone lose sight of the sun for months? I mean, think of the mystery hidden in its slippery gems, of the sweetness of the tongue sealing the union with the beloved in the Song of Songs. And I succumb, despite how messy it is to crack the fruits open, invade that hive, oblivious to the indelible droplets splattering the sink, reaching beyond the marble counter all over my arms and face, as my fingertips delicately remove its inner membranes, until the bowl is filled with shiny ruby red arils. I add a few drops of rose and orange blossom water, the way my mother did, and my grandmother used to do, and her mother before her.

The Upright Piano

I see myself out in the cold, draped in a silk nightgown, seated barefoot on a stool by that upright piano, you know, the one my mother bought when she thought I should take piano lessons, while others played during recess, oh, how I first struggled striking notes daily, practicing scales, then rehearsing Mozart's "Rondo alla Turca" till I'd play it in my mind relentlessly, *tan tan tan . . . tan tan tan . . .* even when I knew I'd never learn another piece, and now, half a century later, I am drawing with memory's wavering lines that same piano to make it the vessel of my heart's message, of so much left unsaid buried in a bitter well turning into notes that rise in tongues of cold fire licking my insides with every key I touch, unharmed, I feel the piano ablaze under my fingertips, twisted candles adorn its top that grows into a tower and turrets spouting flames from windows, a menace to the adjacent branches, my fingers wildly strike the keyboard while the sky opens up like a stage filled with shimmering damask memories dancing to the melody like maddened fireflies.

Nocturne

While all passengers are asleep, I stay up late, bent over my desk until, rising from the next-door cabin, the woman's voice begins to lull her child to sleep, attentive to the rise and fall of her voice my pencil runs over the page, in a sinuous way echoing the sound of her humming carrying the stories she will surely tell her child when he grows older but that for now are rocking him in the manner of an empty score filled with inaudible words like notes traced with invisible ink only perceived by me who records them faithfully night after night, stringing words and sound waves together as though weaving a necklace in an unknown language drowning her child's cries and nightly fears within reefs filled with corals and thick-lipped butterfly fish kissing away the sadness and longing for the home they left behind and the pains yet to come.

The Memory of Unspoken Words

She has landed on the deck of an abandoned wreck, fails to remember how she swallowed the fiery ball that pulled her like a tidal wave into the stillness of a metallic sky steeped in lavender where angry clouds hover around the drowning sun suffused with coral. Her pillow is a melted cloud filled with birds that forgot how to fly and now swim in a pool that overflows the deck, washing the souls of dead sailors from every leak and corner. She presses on her eyelids to find a different ending to their story, sees her body glow with scales and the fish in the pool grow wings. She knows every drop of water will vanish at dawn, erasing with black ink her luminous shape, alive only in the formless night, and the rainbow will soon shine over a boat with discarded bags heavy with the stained memory of unspoken words and broken planks.

Musical Score in Pearly Layers

A gigantic snail sailing in the brume over misty grass stops, smothered by the haze: or did the cello's music refrain his slimy progression? Head tilted, the mollusk seems only attentive to his vibrant antennae while the man seated on a folding chair embraces his instrument and desperate notes rise, spiraling through the coiled corridors of the voluminous shell, oblivious of the bike left to the care of the tall cello case standing like a Swiss guard. The cellist thinks himself a sailor about to climb into a caravel, flaunting its aerial antennae as a prow, while his bow strums strings in circular motion, sound waves swell, resonate inside the convoluted chambers, searching for the apex of the shell, where the snail's heart beats. Suddenly notes grow wings, leave the musical score, fly freely in flocks around the raised translucent wands guiding their flight.

On the Sargasso Sea

Think of a houseboat floating over a sea of foaming moss so thick
it seems anchored in green dunes despite its full-blown drift though
it's only a contrivance and whoever lives in it is obsessed with the
passing of time: an alarm clock by the bed, a cuckoo at the entrance,
a sundial at the threshold, a timer by the stove, a wooden clock on
the dining table, an hourglass cresting the wall, a bell by the water
clock, and let us not forget the telescope placed between the bottle
of wine and the grapes, stalking the movement of stars.

Grains of sand fall, a rhythm espousing the ticking of clocks: chimes
and bells oscillate, muffled by surrounding haze, and there's no room
for fantasy: its dweller watches coffee drip drop by drop, is aware
how long it takes to read each line on a page, successive seconds
pervade his sleep, even his daydreams, nothing's left to chance, only
he knows deep inside he has become a clock within a clock, afraid
of losing track; lost in that sea of moss, he'd still feel the thump of
his own heartbeat.

Lidless Eyes

It all happened after a furtive tear trickled down followed by a larger one, raindrops of blue sorrow forming a puddle then a pool, drowning me and my unborn child, or was I diving into the deepest of my eyes, undulating in the aqueous humor, eyes wide open, staring at my baby's crib suspended in oceanic blue by a long, stemmed lotus flower sprouting from its center as an umbilical chord rising towards this iridescent parachute unfolding its pearled petals in sympathy, and even medusas wearing their mourning coat slide like a procession of black umbrellas, a silent omen while anemones' lidless eyes stare at me as one of their own.

Drop by Drop

My temples stream with cold sweat like the walls of a subterranean
cave, I need air, my heart spins, grows into a spiral, becomes
petrified into a shell sealed around a Mayan cenote, a deep green
pool filled with the mute echo of sacrificial virgins' sighs: my dreams
drown within the ashes of my memories, with dry eyes, I taste the
salt of swollen tears as they flow away in an eternal drip, infiltrating
through the fissures of mother of pearl: valves burst into a gigantic
wave, propelling me out of myself over foam-covered dunes.

Face à face

When with eyes closed, I face the mirror of desolation, I see myself
as a dove fluttering in slow motion like a still mirage while I walk the
desert dunes, wondering where I'd last seen the scarce palm trees still
erect by the smothered tents where all the ones I've ever loved are
now buried. I search for ashes shrouded in sand, and only see
through half-open lids feathers the color of my hair, lidless eyes
staring at their mirrorless reflection, lips pursed in triangular silence,
and oh, yes, how can I omit those metallic blue shades making us all
one, woman and fowl, in love and loss?

Unborn

I have no eyes, no ears, no lips, a flower drawn from the wild seed of their eyes, elytra's spark in the darkening riverbed, a trembling protean flame rising from an elusive space where skin meets skin. Hand in hand, they watch me grow tongues of flame licking the warm air, extending like fingers in a glove, intertwined vines blossoming in fiery petals. They hear the rustling of dry leaves nearby, a droplet bursting on a tin gutter, a crack in the icy roof, a tear of melting snow, read the sudden silence of wind chimes, hear me whisper: yes, I am, I know . . .

II.

Initiation

Archeological Reminiscence

Once, my son, these plains were swaying with golden wheat, purple hues would appear after seasonal rains as a prayer for harvest. Now the horizon has become deeply dyed in laundry blue, the day seems steeped in vivid aquamarine, as though the sea had decided to look upon us from above. Across the valley stands the colossal sculptures of a man and a woman head bent from time immemorial, a petrified proof of what mankind was able to achieve. Since then no drops of water have fallen, no seed has unfolded its wings, there are no longer workers bent in the fields, only these remnants of a past when we could eat from our sweat. Now we rely on words unsaid, stilled by colors, only allowed to move when lights are out in the gallery, condemned to observe the barrenness Dalí created around us.

Come, son, we shall circle the human ruins, hand in hand, rest under the coolness of their elongated shadow: we can enter the arched doors and climb the inner stairs to enjoy the breathtaking view from the man's hollow heart and the woman's generous thighs, even reach higher into the curve of her hands held like a vessel gathering dew for the birds that nest in the fissures of the stones. See my son, only now can we move freely about the canvas. Let's follow that fragile light filtered through the cerulean canopy; see how it leads the way to the inviting doors? Let's hurry before life resumes in the hallways and someone notices our absence.

Broken Ladder

I am no longer this little boy who ran away at night to milk the moon and stars. What am I to do if the ladder is broken, leaving golden threads dangling in broad daylight, braided rays of hardened light yet fine as silk spun by a silkworm, once linking me to that lost site of fearless joys? But I will send back the stardust I fed on for so long. Now you know why I study the Almanac, awaiting for the right day and time when wheat is ripe, reaching high into those rays of light. You know why I'm here, in the midst of this field, dressed in my Sunday clothes: I will pull these gilded chords as those of a tower bell ringing above beckoning a gift filled with the substance of dreams, wrapped with Queen Mab's veils. Don't fear it is too heavy: it weighs less than a breath or a sigh. Let the wind blow softly, watch it rise to the top with your eyes closed.

Origin

I have no name, no face, no age. I have lost track of my birthplace: a grain of sand blown by the slightest breeze, I've crossed continents and shores, flown over dunes and quarries, known the brush of leaves and grass, even rested in ponds after being swept by crested tides, always unseen, but never lonely, my edges softened by rubbing against ruby, garnet, coral, quartz, shells, endlessly smoothing each other's skin, surviving the heat of scorching sun drowning in carmine sea until that last sacrifice on the pyre where our blood melts into layers and layers of crimson petals opening up in their last frozen gesture. Is anyone aware that I am forever prisoner in that translucent flower?

Desert Song

It all started when he set out in his suit and tie, searching for a sand rose in the desert. Wandering through dream's thresholds, he hoped to unearth a treasure that would resist the drought of feelings, each millenary facet telling of the innumerable ways love can be immortalized. He must have taken a wrong turn since all he found, erect like a menhir, was a fossil. Was it the hip of a dinosaur, or rather a Titan's, lost from times beyond memory, so smoothed by the scorching sun that it bore no signs? Looking closely he saw an open jaw with pointed teeth and a hole where an eye once stared. He feared he had to return empty handed in time for his date, but realized with terror that he had no recollection of the path that led him there.

Inner Voice

With bear coats thrown over her shoulders, she no longer fears the biting winds. Yet, she wears the mahogany weight like an unwanted fragrance. Only she can hear the deafening roar of the wounded animals and their last sigh as they shed their soul like molten skin. She dreams their agony night after night and in a half sleep, sees herself clothed in a homespun gown loosely folded on her chest, baring her full breasts. In her deepest dreams she yearns for large hands to espouse her nakedness.

Forever flanked by two invisible bears thundering in her ears, she errs in the wilderness, desolate, from one mirage to another, unable to deafen an inner voice striving to open her up like a bud, urging her to throw away cloak and pelt. Fully awake, her stride has steadied. Can't you see? She now realizes she has become the bearer of an ancestral wisdom inherent in the feathery dandelion she holds in her hand like a scepter. She knows she can follow the path of every silk-winged seed.

Behind the Scenes

At first glance you might think she is an actress, or a singer standing on stage by an empty cardboard house, a still backdrop of course, until a waft of wind blows across the curtain, a *trompe-l'œil* creating the illusion of life. Yet you can see, seeping through the wide-open windows, the colors of her beating heart while she is hiding her mood behind a white enigmatic mask, a persona that allows her to meditate before the performance. Is her dress woven with the fabric of clouds and silvery scales? But if you look more closely you'll see she is emerging from a sea made of the condensation of the evening sky, a crescent moon adorns her chest, a school of fish circles her breasts and thighs, her arms and torso are just being painted, she is only part of the unfinished background.

Afterthought

If she weren't stilled by the painter's gaze, cast by John William
Waterhouse in the role of Lamia kneeling in front of an unidentified
knight posing as young Lycius, she would tell him how he once lit a
candle within her that resisted melting, a magical trick or a spell, since
the flame grew even when he'd look at her sideways unknowing
what step to take, waiting for her to take the reins as at a crossroads.
He didn't love her, he said, but when alone in the coupé, weren't his
knees shaking, shaking the seat, shaking her heart? Weren't his lips
thinking this is not happening, while her lips tasted their unraveled
silkiness? And was he responsible for the spurned flame that still
burns on an invisible wick, stretches and shrinks in a ritual dance? Was
he ever aware that under her eyelids a shadow show lit keeps
growing stronger day by day?

Brushstrokes

Without any sound, waves permeate the floor, algae cover the curtains with an insidious verdigris patina, and she watches herself, complacent, looking awry in the mirror while she unbuttons her black evening dress, a mirror that remains empty like her own life. Seated in a sofa, back turned, he drowns in his indifference into the surge, and surely, it is his face that is seen reflected in the portrait hanging on the wall, an immersed look, barely visible behind the wide-open newspaper. Waters rise to the rhythm of the notes resounding from the rear window, in which a man with a white wig plays the piano, as though it were Mozart composing his Requiem. The painter raises inexorably the level of the waters, and the woman knows that even in that last moment, she will only be fulfilled by drowning in the torrent furtively surrounding them.

The Ages of Man

She lives with a man she now softly calls a living dead, fingers
covering her lips like a feathered fan, she barely proffers these words,
feels trapped, yes, as walls shrink around her, getting closer each day.
She, who never had children, is nursing her no-longer lover. Always
by his side, rubbing his failing limbs, calming his speeding pulse. He
has aged so much after his illness, she thinks, watches how his skin
fails to wrap the bones, hanging in places like the folds of a handed
down garment. He suddenly awakens at night anguished, fears the
sandman, needs to lie next to her and hold her hand. She dreams of
opening the door wide-open, of stepping out to the light, to an
uninterrupted sleep.

Awakening

Rising earlier each day, the young girl watches dawn budding in
warm colors through the lace-curtain veils covering her window. She
opens her hand to stop the light beam piercing the semi darkness,
yearns to touch the glimmering motes of dust, watches her fingers
become transparent, a white glowing lining surrounding them, thinks
of anemones' fingers playing an invisible underwater instrument as
notes fill the space, turn into words rushing from every corner,
crowding the room. She senses the air has become dense, heavier:
she moves slowly as though in a dry aquarium while her one-eyed
fingers grow in size, gaze through the window as the walls close in
on her, enveloping like a tidal wave.

The Ages of Woman

The three-way mirror refuses to reflect her tattered dress, the withered flower falling from her startled hand as she sees the bride she once was, seated on the throne of youth, as in a centerfold, holding a lily, erect like a scepter in her right hand, the other grasping a bouquet over her lap, unaware of crossing oceans of time about to overflow, their white-crested waves already reaching the commode where the circular clock stopped ticking.

And the left and right panes of the mirror remain blank as past and future merge, there is no reflection of the old woman's tired self, her thinning hair. She gazes at the image facing her with a doe's frightened stare, feels sorry for the girl seated on the throne of youth, smiles at her own knotted hands and swollen veins that tell stories the girl cannot understand.

She has so much to say, she thinks, notices the fallen hour hands nearby. She has time till waters rise up to her knees; soon they will all disappear in the storytelling. The old woman could leave the room, restart the clock, stop the illusion, but it is her chance to speak to a captive audience, to say goodbye.

Walking Around in Cambodia

She faces the ruins of a temple intertwined with secular trunks filled with echoes of footsteps and wings flapping, hears muffled voices through interstices where tall blades of grass sprout, finding their way into every crevice. She'd like to experience passion this way, the way the divided trunk espouses stones with ligneous arms, the way vines' fingertips fumble through every fissure, every open space, in a perpetual embrace, thinks of how her fingers run through her hair when she braids and unbraids her rebellious locks, imagines the way each spear grows, filling with its presence every unseen gap in the dried bark striated with deep wrinkles calling for dew.

She marvels at these excoriated stones skinned over and over, now densely covered with moss, the moss of forgetfulness, and wonders how no force could prevent the symbiosis between wooden fibers and mineral grain, annulling the slightest openness, silencing moans, erasing witnesses. She thinks of cracks and scars in a string of relationships, vestiges gathered in a yellowing photo album, once erected, now forgotten in an attic, pages glued with humidity, covered with mildew. Would erosion after erosion have erased the memory of how much blood was spilled to build these monuments, to keep them alive?

Gezi Park, 2013

When bulldozers rolled on, poems of protest covered the walls

At nightfall, they melt into a sea of discontent, glide like a procession
of fireflies answering the same call. Invisible hands hold a flickering
candle, feet stomp ebony streets, at times, a face appears outlined like
a picture and its negative.

Staring through windowpanes and balconies, eyes follow the silent
march. Flames rise, scintillate under streetlights. Each tiny flame, a
prayer for trees to breathe in the heart of the city where voices are
heard riding the wind, where whispers seep through rustling leaves,
reach benches where lovers hold hands, spin around street artists,
pause by storytellers, into children's curls, before landing on the
forgotten newspaper where words in suspension gather strength.

And the roots remember, strong rhizomes stretch elastic limbs, new
shoots yawn awakened by dawn, echoing millenary murmurs.

III.

Hiding Under Brushstrokes

One thing was constant in her composition,
      a couple sitting on a bench under a palm tree,
      a mimosa or even an oleander.

She once thought she'd place them
by a thatched cottage
      disappearing under magenta bougainvilleas
      surrounded with elms or willows
            silver strands swaying at the slightest breeze . . .

but where would she locate this *locus amoenus,*
in a suburb or the countryside?

With time, she settled for an apartment,
      or a small roof-garden,
then only four walls framing distant silhouettes.

She chose oils. This way, no one would see the flaws . . .
      just let the paint dry, then improvise,

      covering layer after layer of burnt sienna, ochre,
      or raw umber with clouds of cobalt blue,
         indigo or cerulean,
            changing seasons at will.

Watercolors were out of the question,
each brushstroke,
each empty space
      revealed the flight of a thought,
      the unspoken word,
         an unfinished sentence . . .

Could one ever place words in people's mouths,
color their mind or heart?
      What if they never look straight into your eyes?

The way the trace
of a fingertip on a butterfly's wing could not be mended,
the stain on the paper echoes

       a word misunderstood,
another overheard,
  a twist of the lips,
          the back of a shoulder.

She'd stack sketches on shelves,
folded in two or four like folios,
       maybe rolled papyrus-like
         full of a mute tumult behind closed doors,
often read between shades when open folds
released rays of moonlight
       captured through lowered blinds.

But with oils, only one canvas was enough
         a palimpsest that could last forever
layer over layer forming a three-dimensional
painting of an empty square
           she alone could decipher . . .

She meditated hours long facing that perfect
shape enclosing a circular mandala,
       a soothing sight
she framed as her final version

until the frame stretched,
       matching the size of her own walls,
          merging with the gilded magenta wallpaper.

A Triptych,

Visibile Parlare in Sotto Voce

I. What the Painter Hears

A Song from the Viennese, Whispered to Klimt

You wanted our encounter to be a ritual,
      planned every detail:
         Ivy circled your hair,
   I interlaced mine
 with violets and jasmine.
Wrapped in a diaphanous sarong,
    I stood by the bed of forget-me-nots.
      You held me
against your silk kimono,
        the sun's folded wings framed us
    in its golden coin.
Losing my balance, I fell on my knees,
    clinging to you,
       my arm around your bent shoulder.
Eyes closed, I could see your hands
      cupped around my face
as if holding a precious porcelain.
   I pressed my toes
     against the ground
 afraid we'd sink
     into the abyss,
both trapped within one trunk,
     one womb,
as if you were my own
    and I, Mother Earth bearing fruit,
     merging our beginnings.
Let me become that space
    between your palms,
the mark of your lips on my cheek.

II. The Artist as Voyeur

Schiele's Glimpse at Love

I want them to hold each other as if it were their last embrace.
It is unusual, I know, for anyone to witness such fiery tenderness
but long to see desire itself as I've always dreamt it,
not as I saw it in eyes saddened by layers of Kohl and mascara.
Isn't it what the child in us seeks,
to be one with the primal act of one's conception?

I want to forget the circled eyes of children consumed
by their own fire, their pupil, the color of pain and loneliness . . .
So I tell my models not to delay this embrace. They undress clumsily,
hug each other so tightly they can't breathe. His arms pressed
around her waist crush her, yet she should not feel the pain,
for what is pain if not of longing, or letting go?

~

I want her hair to cascade in deep green over the white folds
of wrinkled sheets framing their face: let it fall on the nape of his neck,
let him sense her sweet fragrance. I want him to wish he'd drown
in their dark waters, in the depths of scenes rushing into his mind,
of her of him of them of then of now all at once.

I want to be part of his vision, wish I could paint myself in his place,
feel images flow from her skin to mine. I turn the hour hand back,
and over moonless waters in the darkness of a womblike warmth,
I glimpse my own reflection in their surrender,
the desire of myself dissolving time and space.

~

Her fingers run over his shoulder, digging nails into his flesh
as if writing on clay, a clay I have become, for I know too well how
she remodels his chin, his lips, his cheekbone, her fingertips rest
in the crease of his earlobe, giving me time to paint, to imagine how
she remodels my chin, my lips, my cheekbone, her fingertips resting
in the crease of my earlobe as I draw myself onto them.

My back overlaps his, as my body and hers become one
with every stroke. She forgets him, a mere screen for this séance
to take place. He whispers through her hair, but I know
she only hears my brushstrokes thrusting her face into her shoulder
as if trying to silence her, forcing her to bite her own flesh.
I know she will later read my unwritten words on the canvas.
Does she notice how his voice is now covered by the sound of my brush?

~

I paint myself as I paint them, a day at a time, my words suffused
in linseed oil muffle even their thoughts, seep through sheets,
beneath wavy curls, fold white curves around her body, between her legs.
She opens up like a flower offering more surfaces to the wind.
As I press the tip of the brush, I hear them think in Braille.
My palette feels heavier, the session is over. They dress up
like empty shells, leave me facing Us in a *visibile parlare,*
She and I, in such an embrace, I will never recapture.

III. Before the Storm

The Wind Trapped by Kokoschka, Rests by his Bride

He lies eyes wide-open, brows tense,
    lips pressed together,
his rugged hands
    knotted over his belly as if in pain.
        They have just made love,
their bodies' tide lulled her to sleep,
    and soon, they'd be swept away
in a whirlwind . . .
     yet she sleeps unaware,
    lost in enchanted woods
while he senses the gust   miles away,
    hears murmurs   in the thickets,
    feels ripples formed
by frightened wings.
   Head leaning on his shoulder,
    a closed fist against his chest,
her dreams speak in tongues,
  in her faint smile . . .
    under her lowered eyelids.

~

He remembers how she'd wait for him:
  in the clearings   at her doorstep,
    by the circular fountain
beneath tall beech trees.
    He'd watch her read omens
in their bark's charcoaled eyes,
    outline her profile . . .

a medallion in evening sepia,
see her dress   tremble
at the slightest breeze;
   he'd enter the courtyard,
      rush through dark corridors,
         drape himself with her smell
till she'd bend under his weight.

~

As though lying in tall branches,
      they feel the rustle of leaves,
         the sway of sycamores, imposing pines.
   He has to leave without looking back,
   join forces with the North wind,
      break the reflection captured in her eyes.
         Could he ever explain he was just
            the substance of her dreams?
      She would wake up soon,
         the fury of the storm deafening,
      its call   irresistible,
            erasing the mirage of her shadow.
               He thinks of getting up but cannot move . . .
the painter's gaze anchoring him by her side.

Goya Dining at *La Quinta del Sordo*

The House of the Deaf Man

Draperies cover your painted walls
for fear of the Inquisition's eyes.
Each night, your servants unveil
the scenes that accompany
your candlelight supper.

Do you rejoice in watching
the wavering flame stretch faces
and shadows, adding depth
to the grotesque figures?

The Sabbath witches' whispers
only you can hear,
reach you
through your deafness.

No longer "*el sordo*," your eyes
sense every complaint, every motion,
the grinding of Saturn's teeth
devouring his son's limbs,

the brittlest cracked bone
echoes your own munching
on a drumstick.

Is it that only the half tones
cast by Promethean flames
enable you to confront the real face
of war, famine and greed?

Night after night you defy intolerance,
revel in a distorted vision
of your somber thoughts.

For if seen in broad daylight,
as would Dorian Gray in later years,
facing his secret portrait's transformation,
you might die of shame.

Walking Around Bernini's *Apollo & Daphne*

Borghese Gallery

You can feel the wind in their faces,
lifting their clothes.
Frozen in flight, bodies strung,
unable to surrender,
his hand on her waist
is the closest to possession.

Stretched between earth and sky,
her raised arms reach
the highest leaves,
feet anchored, veins
merge in a web of darkness

as her skin hardens
under his touch,
she yearns to feel a while longer
the warmth invading
a body no longer hers,
enveloping

like breeze through long curls,
numbing her steps,
face leaning towards
her pursuer, eyes lowered,
looking back in vain,

unable to contemplate the cause
of her change,
sadness
fills her with its sap.

Lovers,

in *The Garden of Earthly Delights*

They have taken refuge in a transparent
sphere in the midst of nudes riding
unicorns, gryphons and camels, reveling
among gigantic birds and berries.

Seen through the slightly opaque screen,
their bodies seem ethereal, a silent
reproval of the orgy of sepias, pinks
and reds around them.

From a distance, the cracked glass recalls
a crystal egg about to hatch, a veined
butterfly's wing nestled in a voluminous
black flower.

Or are the lovers seated inside a dewdrop
blown from a gold-petalled mouth, born
from a flower's heart?

In their greenhouse, they barely move,
fearful of tearing the diaphanous veil.

He stares to her right, his breath flowing
on the nape of her neck, a gentle stroke
on her belly, a wish or promise for a
child to come.

Eyes half-closed, she dreams of bearing
his child. Her heart sings the *Magnificat*
at her lover's touch. Rejoicing he is no
Archangel, she rests a hand on his knee.

They hide, still, cautious. Anything could
destroy the invisible net setting them apart,
the brightest spot on the canvas.

Words, even love words, can have sharp edges,
distend the perfect shape. Their hands, lovers'
winged fingers, speak in a motionless caress.

Inside your Palm

Rehearsal of a Ballet

No one pays attention
            to you anymore
when you paint backstage standing
        in the dark wings
                or sketch from the orchestra stalls.
        I see you
        in the shadows
                    defining a silhouette
as I try to follow your brushstrokes,
            my canvas comes to life,
                —you laugh at my hesitant steps.

With eyes closed,
            you know where
a *cabriole* would land,
        capture
                    the arc of a *pirouette*,
                    the play of light over fingers
                            tying grosgrain lace,
                    the trembling of a *tutu*
                    held inside your palm,
its white tulle flowing in mid-air
                —an eerie parachute.

You sense the stiffness
            of a dancer's shoulders
stretching on the wooden floor
        as she rearranges
                    the black velvet ribbon
            at the nape of her neck,
        another, arms crossed
    behind her back
                —sighs deeply.

Some press their toes down
                to ensure the grip of the shoe.

                In the backdrop,
            emerging in *chiaroscuro*,
                        faces & busts
                lean against
giant cardboard ferns
                —tired butterflies at dusk.

With the tip of your brush,
            you slow their heartbeat
                        till the conductor's wand
            signals the movement,
                        steps espouse
the musical phrase.
Your gaze lingers
            over the vivid colors
on your palette as though
            the ballerinas on stage were
                        a simulacra
                        —an echo of your own vision

At night, you follow them
                on their way home,
            each humming a tune, hurrying
                on the slippery pavement
                        under Parisian drizzle, awkward
            on leather *bottines*—swans on dry land
carrying satin shoes on their backs
            —like spare wings.

You enter their dream
pas de deux, de quatre . . .
     their legs scissor
          back and forth
. . . notes climb ladders formed
     by the lines of a score,
         crowding spaces
              in counterpoint,
             hopping *en pointe*,
    on one foot
         —like winged ants.

IV.

Mona Lisa

In my efforts to escape
I often enter a portrait.
Now I am the Mona Lisa
sealed by deft brushstrokes
framed in my mind—
a captured image, a shelter
to isolate myself and sink within
the space of an outlined smile.

Reading at a Table

After Picasso

Head bent over an open book, she sees her hands become wings,
rustle through the leaves, caress her forehead in a flight in still motion
while her head splits as she reads two pages at a time, frontward
backwards, rehearses the plot, rewrites the story, lips half-open. Her
smile brightens the pale fire rising from the flame trapped inside the
lampshade; its ebb and flow casts a faint light over the man in the
background draped in a tropical robe, a puppy held against his chest,
both faces encased tesserae, the glow sealing them within gold leaf.
Mouth agape, the woman doesn't notice how her table shrinks, how
her hand flutters faster. Her feathered fingers erase distances, write in
the margins, words dance under the hollow shaft that is her wrist.
She finds herself writing in the book's blank pages: her calamus fills
leaf after leaf with signs guided by the master's brush. Her smile is a
sliver of moon now lined in liquid gold like the wild flowers in her
hair trapped in a mosaic of dreams.

The Captive

Immobilized by pigments and glaze for so long, I emerged, colors
melting around my fingers, the canvas fibers disintegrating, freeing
me at last. I find myself alive, fingering Tarot cards, one by one:
endowed now with divination powers, I no longer need the Fool,
nor the Sun. With each flipped card, I gain sight into a different
dimension, face my double across the empty frame, staring at me
and at its shadow while I watch my own shadow grow over the
woman's shoulders, palms outstretched, turning into big clouds
projecting an arcane ink and wash landscape over the white lace of
her panties.

The Camisole

The silk fabric slides between my fingers, I still feel the softness of its essential oils, permeating my skin, pungent and smooth as though I'd woven it just for you with spikes harvested from endless lavender fields in Provence, or as though I were a silk worm raised on lavender petals, and I'd spun that silken thread to wrap around me when you'd finally come, all that and more I dreamt of offering you, year after year, and here we are, that is, my camisole and I, waiting for you in the silence of that hotel room.

Under the Crescent Moon

The violinist has grown wings,
the donkey is flying.
The bride and groom listen all night long
to the blue notes cascading over the red-tiled roof.

They hear a secret tune,
each from a different slice of the moon.

He takes off his top hat, unties his black knot,
hums to the opalescence marking
the beginning of his dance.

Dovelike, she lies in embroidered sheets,
her ruffled dress rests on a chair like discarded wings.
She knows her waist will swell by the full moon,
dreams of its dark side where Chagall is hiding.

Sounds in the Attic

Fluttering wings wrapped in shimmering muslin veils dance around
the broken planks, a gaping wound in the hardwood floor littered
with scattered down, love letters flying away from torn photographs.
A whisper breaks the rhythm of the footbeats: a tree is unearthed, its
roots bleed, veins sapping roots of my heart, throbbing as a
frightened sparrow held tightly in a palm. Hungry moon, do not lure
me into your maddened circle. Don't you see that hole in my chest
no longer keeps a beat?

Shipwrecked

Her body sinks into the wavy sheets, the sea of down calming after
the assault, the raging battle of the senses leaving her inert, absent, her
thighs ripe and fragrant, a guava still reeking of our mixed juices:
time after time we have risen from the abyss, empty carcasses lying
on a raft of bitterness. Why this urge to go down the stairs, press on
the accelerator? Only then does my hand measure the heaviness of
her breasts, correct the choreography of each gesture, motion her to
dress and undress as I compose a montage of my favorite stills, like
a child playing at forbidden games, I want to do it all at once, merge
the end with the beginning, yes, she sighs, you have touched my soul,
melts into a mirror of water: a star quivers, I lose myself in the
middle of its eye while we drown in the waves we create: there's no
ocean to sate my thirst until I face the wrinkled sheets weighing on
me and want to leave again.

Skin Flashing Where the Garment Gapes

A water sculpture, a spring erect in the shape of a woman, fluid as a mirror held to the awakening sycamores, soothing their albescent knots and twisted joints under shedding flakes of bark. Can't you feel the moisture in her curves? At first glance you might think her about to bathe in the clear pool by the blue stones, but truly she is made of water and rose from it, a teaser slowly dropping an illusion of a wraparound garment that is really a sheet of water, still unable to break down and become woman, she projects her image over the young man lying down on the smooth rocks, face leaning on his bent elbow, he watches her appear and disappear, the sheets of water vanishing into mist in the early hours, stares at her skin flashing where the garment gapes, oscillating between life and death.

The Dance

You once taught me the geometry of music, how every musical
phrase melts into lines, twists and turns, curves and shapes broken by
sound: In awe, I watched you read the astrolabe to tell the rising and
setting times of the sun. Partners for so long on that dancing floor,
we glide with apparent ease over its mosaic configurations, arguing
constantly while our bodies, oblivious of words' rough edges hissing
like serpents coiled in our ears, make us spin as though our feet were
clad in shoes with a mind of their own. Architect of our sempiternal
altercations, you measure with angular rectitude the slightest sway:
isn't a swing for you but a simple equation, our motion, an inverted
pendulum? You take the lead, I follow. Forced to play by your rules,
unwilling to hold a ruler straight, I saw you draw pointed angles that
stop the heart from beating: with time, I've learned to slide over lines
and hide in corners. I will not be the shadow of your pendulum.

Insomnia in Sorrento

We walk on the soft humid sand, shining under the moonlight,
see our footsteps disappear like words afraid to touch our skin.
We sip our *limoncello* certain that the moon squeezed itself
in each glass, rich and pulpous, oozing zest. We hear the seagulls
cry in the dark, screeching like alley cats mating. Warm waves
lather our feet, foam lightens the volcanic black soil. I think of
our visit this morning to the lemon grove, how we ran our fingers
over the rugged globes' scented skin while trees grow around us,
circling us, pregnant moons hanging from their branches.

V.

Under the Waterfall

It all began on a Summer solstice dawn: the sun disappeared in a fiery sky of molten marigolds and blood flowers tainting misty waterfalls all the way to the swan cove. And the startled swans wandered around mounds of featherless flesh lying pell-mell, sleeping forms with sparse down crowning their heads, a burnt umber field of sepia limbs sprouting from broken shells, their strange, acrid smell, terrified them: flapping their immaculate wings, they kept bathing in the purifying waters, came back to the inert bodies in maddened circles biting their own tails amidst the dormant newborns: had they heard of Andersen's tales they'd wonder why they were all cursed at once with ugly little ducklings, unaware they were witnessing the origin of the human race.

Boreas' Anger

After giant waves whipped the rocky shoreline devouring cliffs at its passage, what seemed from a distance a snail hovering over a rock drifting like cork, or small islands bobbing over the dark waters has filled my heart with consternation as I realize these volutes of smoke billowing up all over like messages of distress appear now to be fumes spewed by the combustion of sins, the world turned upside down, and I who yearned to rescue, set out in my small skiff searching for life on coral islands, ventured so close I can see this giant hovering snaillike figure blowing, alimenting the furnace, with his metal face forged by Hades and all I can do is lower my head in consternation but do not mistake me for Charon, and note that my companion has only one head.

Encounter in the Yellow Hour

You'd think we're about to engage in an elegant minuet, right hands
raised in the ritual sequence of honor, yet her left hand waves the
bouquet of wildflowers away from me as mine struggles to hold
down my vest blown by the wind: but wait, rewind the tape to when
I first saw her walking towards me, as though floating in that sea of
wheat, holding wildflowers gathered just for me, for she must have
mistaken me from afar for a pirate with my kilt and wide-brimmed
hat: how I fooled myself, falling into my own trap, a motionless
ready-made, unable to take her into high seas like a one-legged sailor,
nor make love to her in the golden swaying waves of wheat, I, the
trickster would-be scarecrow won't come to life like the fairy tale
frog, even the scorching heat won't cast away my self-inflicted spell:
this is the end of the minuet, the last farewell steps of the ritual
sequence of honor, she'll let the flowers scatter in the wind, the still
dance lasting for an instant merging end with beginning.

Trompe-l'œil

Don't come any closer little one: did you think me a flower from afar, deceived by the smell of this cloud of fragrant roses circling around me? Their whiteness I bore once when my body was ethereal: I am no longer a painted cloud that looks like a rose, but a woman wearing the horned symbols of power erect like pistils: don't you see I bear no nectar to refuel your flight path? Face covered with tar I will lead the procession when my sisters' spirits will join me, trading their floating whiteness for flesh and blood, rebelling against the gatherers of flowers who must now bow to us: we will harvest them whenever ready to bear their fruits and no longer be their carpe diem.

The Canary & the Feathered Mask

How many birds' blood was spilled so that you would come to life,
a monstrous mixture of Aztec headdress and Venetian inlaid gold,
oftentimes an accomplice of heaven knows how many infamous
plots hidden beneath twisted features. Now you lie, abandoned in a
corner of this shelf, empty, useless, while I stare at you with scorn: a
simulacrum, your motionless feathers serve no purpose: can you
spread your wings in flight, double your own volume while singing
or dance as you twirl and trill at will? All that blood spilled, fed to
the hungry hearth to shape your semblance, to sharpen the tip of the
biting chisel into that stilted face. I will not sing for you.

Flora & the End of the Bird's Song

Do you think I don't feel spiraling ferns unfurl all over my moss-covered hair, vibrant like a horse's mane, tips brushing over my naked shoulders? Don't you see how pale my skin is from hiding in the shadows of the underwoods, surrounded with silence yet still sensing the growth of each ripening berry, my thoughts mushrooming like foam as I sense slippery serpentine movements and a sudden flutter of wings, both predator and prey feasting on the free meal crowning my head. But why should I feel sorry for the end of the bird's song? Doesn't he also stop the worm from unfolding its butterfly's wings?

Time Off

Zeus once took the shape of a bull, a swan...

The blond girl moans: a petal flowing in her hand like a golden scarf, eyes closed, she reclines her head. She knows this is only the first round. All the giant sunflower lost were a few petals littering the staircase. All the gilded creature could do was tear her dress apart, reveal her pubescent body, her delicate skin now covered with pollen even more desirable to his touch. Nearby, her dark-haired sister's mane is electrified, strands wiggling like cobras. Fists closed, she's ready to fight the tired creature lying still, his multifaceted eye staring, petals erect, stamen reeking with nectar . . . . Do not be fooled. He will attack with renewed strength. Will he steal the kiss of death before her sister opens her eyes?

It Takes Two to Tango

You got it all wrong: no one ever heard my side of the story. I never feared his touch: engaged him in a smooth dance that later on you came to call a tango, facing him straight on, leading him, his weight leaning against my arched body, my hand an iron fist in a velvet glove: let me close my eyes to retrace our steps, yes, feel our feet soaked in Sidon's blue warmth as warm as his breath, and, yes, I placed my flower necklace around his neck, yes, and softly whispered promises in his ear to take me away to other shores that now bear my name, yes, and keep in mind he was not white like Pasiphae's obscure object of desire.

Duel at Dawn

The sky's purple hair turns gray from fear, the lost moon lands on the train's forehead, flooding the racing horse with light. The bronze horse's size is not his forte, he is not hollow, has never heard of Troy: his is the courage of a hundred warriors, their death fueling his speed, he reclaims his ancestors' peaceful plains and pastures. Past and future meet at the railroad: eager to destroy their distorted mirror image, they exhale their purple breath, rush towards inevitable doom in the leaden dawn. The horse is champion to hordes of horses and even with the moon on his side the one-eyed steel monster is still blind. Will the pages turn back? Will one of them survive?

Timing

It all happened so fast, I can still feel his breath, his lips stripping my
will; skin scorched by his touch, I stood, mouth agape, a still syllable
floating in the air, unable to reverse my wish, already caught in a shell
of bark, twigs tying me tighter than handcuffs: through the interstices
of the ligneous fibers, I saw his silhouette fade into the horizon.
How I wished I could turn the hour hand back: had I only known.
And don't you think it's over, I still breathe under my porous mask,
feel sunrays and wafts of warm breeze, and my now awakened
body aches for what might have been. No one seems to know it, but
later, much later, my fate would inspire the torments of Dante's
suicides trapped in gnarled trees, bleeding at the slightest touch,
lamenting the human form they rejected in life.

Expectations

Face to face, standing in an immobile boat, two lovers are enveloped by a lapis lazuli glow as though out of a painting by Miró revisited by Klein: the deep sea evaporates around them, freeing a school of red fish gliding at ease as in an aquarium: only their fins flicker like fireflies around the nascent crescent, a silent witness to that still scene: the boy holds a loaf of moon in one hand while in the other shines a scarlet star, color of the girl's bonnet. Slightly bent over his offerings, she reflects, her crossed hands weighing her breasts heavy with promises and songs.

Phoenician Twilight

The nuptials of sun and moon, a ritual I yearned to witness for so long, sailing aimlessly, watching sunset after sunset, my beard growing grayer, and now that I'm finally near the shores of Tyre and Sidon, where dice were once thrown under a full moon, where wreaths of incense ascended and mingled with the winds of heaven to lead us safely, can I trust what my eyes are seeing? Are the sun and moon really sinking side by side into the darkening waters, or is it my boat, heavier with its load of gold and silver coins, each a sun and a moon, replete with amber, spices and royal purple, riches collected from countless counters, weighing more every minute like my falling eyelids.

At the Violet Hour

Star-crossed lovers unite high above as the city slips into slumber. I alone keep watch at the lighthouse, longing to be swept by the big wave, feel it rolling me in its indigo fingers cooling me into a ball of blue ice, a maddened dervish whirling layers and layers of sea and sky in the ways of the Crazy Redhead who keeps the secret of every stroke, I choose to ignore these black leaping flames springing out of hatred and envy, a bonfire lit with rolled parchments filled with lost dreams and rosemary, its sparks scattering yellow poppies in a cerulean field. How I wish you could see how the timid evening crescent nests inside its golden case.

VI.

After the Storm

Dead trees erect as Dalí's crutches,
hold broken branches in angled joints,
forsaken trophies no one reclaims, tangled
in old vines, disjointed, distorted bones,

elephant skin filled with memories
I wish to rip, fragment, discard, as I pull,
uproot trees still resisting, conjuring
up new shoots, refusing to give up.

I gather strewn twigs like an automaton
in an open-air ossuary revealing desecrated
fossils flown from thickets and tall branches,
pile them up at the farthest end of the creek,

throw them away with all my strength,
watch the arc they form in the air,
see how they land on the other side
in a cemetery of lost illusions.

I reach for a hanging branch with blue patina,
a sunken treasure the color of my dreams,
its hollow, brittle limbs easy to break,
tsik . . . tsik, one by one, tsik . . . tsik . . . tsik . . .

Others, I leave on the side of the paths,
sculptures too heavy to lift, nature's
Petri dishes, grounds for rippled
mushrooms writing their own memoir
in the hidden calligraphy of their folds.

Hokusai's *The Great Wave*

in wake of Fukushima, 2011

It is said Hokusai never intended to represent
a tsunami, but an *okinami*, a wave of the open sea,
erect, foam curling up its claw-crested fingers
over stunned boatmen surfing in reverence.

And I wonder what made that captive wave leap
out, release the dormant creature locked in
for centuries in shades of Prussian blue,
its delicate swirls spewing muddy torrents

over Fukushima's shores, erasing in black ink
all shapes ever drawn, engraved or breathing,
its voracious appetite growing in silence, its heart
melting blackness into the heart of nuclear reactors.

What made it erupt like a maddened volcano
famished for blood, steel teeth crushing tiles, wood,
metal, belching in a roar engulfing homes, cars,
boats, buses, men, women, children, newborn,

unborn, all swept like broken twigs and fallen leaves,
carrying seeds that will not grow for seasons to come.
The wave of the open sea now speaks in tongues,
each curve, a threat, its filigree lines and blue hues

seem steeped in lethal pigments. In the print's empty
spaces, spirits hold their breath, dotted droplets
filled with suffocated, inaudible voices, whisper:

Remember me, I no longer have this beautiful skin.
Remember the light that came out of my eyes.
Remember my story never to be told.
Remember my smile, my hands, my dreams.
Hokusai, your *okinami* has lost its innocence.

After the Tsunami: The Cherry Tree Laments

Hanami is the Japanese celebration
of the ephemeral beauty of sakura, or cherry blossoms

I.

Submerged, as in a dream,
        in an abyss of darkness,
                I found myself
half-buried in silt.

       Or was it a mossy
quagmire?

My world upside down,

           I couldn't breathe or see the sky,
           I couldn't feel the brush of the wind,
           I couldn't hear the flutter of a wing.

      ~

         My roots grew cold. I yearned
            for a ray of sunlight.
How long did my blindness last?

Drowning softly in that black night,
        I wake to a dance
           of floating shadows,

         glaucous eyes,
              ashen,   tumefied faces
stare at the bottomless well.

      ~

Fibrillating fins
                disrobe   mangled
bodies smeared by seaweed,
        sunken shapes entangled in algae's hair.

            Helpless, I sense a cry
        out of the mouth
of a wound   mute syllables waver
            sear shattered lips.

II.

I breathe the newborn scent of earth.
      Is it yet another dream?
           Veins throb inside
my hardened bark.
           Nothing around me   the same.

      No one celebrates *hanami*
under my shade,
          no paper lantern
       quivers in the breeze.

      ~

My weary branches
          heavy with petals,
      fingertips blossoming sighs,

         stories   lost,
fallen petals
      scatter letters
         no child cares   to gather.

      faces flown
like efflorescence
         swept by a strong wind,
bodies
      dispersed by tidal waves.

      ~

I have seen shadows at nightfall
        reclaim   last moments,
                heard trembling voices
      hold a *hanami* of their own.

             My five-petaled flower
lost its scented message,
            only shades speak of transience now,
      only whispers   circle
around   my trunk

Aftershocks in Fukushima

A woman's stride shakes the muddy soil
echoes deep down dark, unseen corridors.
A damp silence clouds the sky.
She walks everyday among shattered
houses, heaps of splintered wood,
looking for her son's body.
She keeps repeating his name.

~

Another squats, burrowing elbow
deep. She looks for her vegetable
garden, invisible under planks, twisted
window sills. Her fingers feel
the roundness of roots, loosen blackened
leeks one by one. They still breathe
unearthed beneath shapeless debris.
She needs water to wash herself.

~

Heteroclite objects flown out of place,
teapots, cups, mirrors, sink, walls turn
into floors bearing unwanted weights.
Scraps of screens call doorknobs neighbors.
Shapeless steel torn like brittle cardboard,
slivers piled-up pell-mell hiding lifeless flesh
vanish in moist sand like abalone shells.
They've lost their shape, their name,
not their memory.

~

A newlywed seated on a bench
clutches her husband's leather jacket.
She rocks it like a baby in her arms
presses it hard onto her chest.
From a rooftop, she saw him drive
up the hill, saw flooding waters rise.
His smell still lingers in the fabric.

~

The old woman is so cold she stopped
feeling her toes. Even her rice cake shivers
wrapped in a frozen aluminum sheet.
She dreams of a warm bowl of soup while
she spoon-feeds her neighbor,
a much older man under diabetes shock.
He needs his medicine.
He needs his diaper changed.

List of Art and Visuals Used as Inspiration

"Afterthought," *Lamia* by John William Waterhouse
"The Ages of Woman," *The Tattered Groom* by Juanita Guccione
"The Artist as Voyeur," *The Embrace* by Egon Schiele
"At the Violet Hour," *Starry Night* by Vincent Van Gogh
"Before the Storm," *Bride of the Wind* by Oskar Kokoschka
"Behind the Scenes," *The Human Element* by Kathleen Kinkopf
"Boreas' Anger," *Metamorphic Awareness (Island of Dead)* by Viktor
    Safonkin
"Broken Ladder," *Lastgeving* by Hans van der Kroef
"Brushstrokes," *Trouble with Time* by Mike Worrall
"The Camisole," *Hotel Room* by Leslie Sealey
"The Canary & the Feathered Mask," *Encounter* by Brian McCarthy
"The Captive," *The Magic Hand* by Charles Rain
"The Dance," *Promise* by Yu Sugawara
"Desert Song," *The Kiss* by Federico Zarco
"Duel at Dawn," *Horse and Train* by Alex Colville
"Encounter in the Yellow Hour," *Meeting* by Gregor Ziolkowski
"*Face à Face*," *Flying Blind* by Jaclyn Alderete
"Flora & the End of the Bird's Song," *Flora with Snake* by Steven Kenny
"Gezi Park, 2013," after photographs of Taksim Gezi Park 2013
    protests by unknown photographers.
"Goya Dining at *La Quinta del Sordo*," *Witches' Sabbath* and *Saturn*
    Devouring His Son by Francisco Goya
"Hokusai's *The Great Wave*," *The Great Wave off Kanagawa* by
    Katsushika Hokusai
"Initiation," *Archeological Reminiscence of Millet's "Angelus"* by Salvador Dalí
"Inner Voice," *The Visible Bears and the Invisible Woman* by Agim Meta
"Inside Your Palm," *The Rehearsal of the Ballet Onstage* by Edgar Degas
"It Takes Two to Tango," *Enticing Europa* by Bill Brauer
"Lidless Eyes," *Who Lit This Flame in Us* by Alexandra Eldridge
"Lovers," *The Garden of Earthly Delights* by Hieronymus Bosch
"The Memory of Unspoken Words," *Siren* by Frédéric Clément
"Mona Lisa," *La Gioconda* by Leonardo da Vinci

HEDY HABRA was born in Egypt and is of Lebanese origin. She is the author of *Tea in Heliopolis*, winner of the 2014 USA Best Book Award for Poetry and finalist for the International Book Award for Poetry, and her collection of short fiction, *Flying Carpets*, won a 2013 Arab American National Book Award's Honorable Mention, and was finalist for the Eric Hoffer Award and the USA Best Book Award. Her book of literary criticism, *Mundos alternos y artísticos en Vargas Llosa*, explores the visual and interartistic elements in the Peruvian novelist's characters' interiority. She has an M.A. and an M.F.A. in English and an M.A. and Ph.D. in Spanish literature, all from Western Michigan University, where she currently teaches and received the All-University Research and Creative Scholar Award and a Doctoral Dissertation Completion Fellowship Award. She is a recipient of the Nazim Hikmet Poetry Award and was finalist for the Pablo Neruda Award. She writes poetry and fiction in French, Spanish, and English and has numerous poems and short stories in journals and anthologies, including *The Bitter Oleander, Blue Fifth Review, Cider Press Review, Connotation Press, Cutthroat, Diode, Drunken Boat, Levure Littéraire, New York Quarterly, Nimrod, Poet Lore, Solstice, Pirene's Fountain, Letras Femeninas, Alba de América* and *Verse Daily*. She has poems forthcoming in *Cimarron Review, Gargoyle* and *World Literature Today*. Her website is HedyHabra.com

www.ingramcontent.com/pod-product-compliance
Lightning Source LLC
LaVergne TN
LVHW041341080426
835512LV00006B/566